D0484191

WORDS TO HELP YOU

BE
STRONG
ALONG THE
PATH OF LIFE

Other Titles in This Series:

Words to Help You
Be a Success

Words to Help You Be Happy
in All the Ways That Matter Most

Words to Help You
Be Positive Every Day

We wish to thank Susan Polis Schutz for permission to reprint the following poems that appear in this publication: "Go beyond yourself and reach..." and "A Friend Is...." Copyright © 1982, 1992 by Stephen Schutz and Susan Polis Schutz. All rights reserved.

Library of Congress Control Number: 2008928041
ISBN: 978-1-59842-252-8

▌┤ and Blue Mountain Press are registered in U.S. Patent and Trademark Office.
Certain trademarks are used under license.

Acknowledgments appear on page 72.

Printed in China.
First Printing: 2008

✪ This book is printed on recycled paper.

This book is printed on fine quality, laid embossed, 80 lb. paper. This paper has been specially produced to be acid free (neutral pH) and contains no groundwood or unbleached pulp. It conforms with the requirements of the American National Standards Institute, Inc., so as to ensure that this book will last and be enjoyed by future generations.

Blue Mountain Arts, Inc.

P.O. Box 4549, Boulder, Colorado 80306

WORDS TO HELP YOU

BE
STRONG
ALONG THE
PATH OF LIFE

Edited by Douglas Pagels

Blue Mountain Press ™

Boulder, Colorado

There's so much strength to be found
in the pages you're about to read...

Introduction

*W*ise words are such wonderful things. Just a few perfect words, spoken or shared at the right time, can change our lives. They can keep us healthy and safe and strong. They can guide us and inspire us. They can teach us how to travel life's path in the best possible way... and avoid some of the problems and pitfalls. They can give us courage. They can give us faith.

Within the pages of this book, you will discover some of the most encouraging and insightful advice you've ever heard. You will be introduced to a number of things you've never read before — but that you'll never forget for as long as you live.

These pearls of wisdom come from a wide variety of remarkable people who share a common message. They believe in being strong, in choosing wisely, and in making each day as rewarding as it can possibly be.

Listen to their conversation, take their messages to heart, and let their words help you be strong... as you continue on your journey through life.

— *Douglas Pagels*

Remember...

Your presence is a present to the world.
You're unique and one of a kind.
Your life can be what you want it to be.
Take the days just one at a time.

Count your blessings, not your troubles.
You'll make it through
    whatever comes along.
Within you are so many answers.
Understand, have courage, be strong.

— *Douglas Pagels*

Words to Reflect On

Even when times are tough, you must never forget what a treasure you are. That special person in the mirror may not always get to hear all the compliments you deserve, but remember… you are so worthy of such an abundance of friendship, joy, and love.

— *Douglas Pagels*

Life is like a mirror; if you frown at it, it frowns back. If you smile, it returns the greeting.

— *W. M. Thackeray*

$\mathcal{I}$ keep a little saying on my mirror that I read every morning and evening. It says, "I am creative, I am powerful, and I can handle it." Obviously there are times when I feel confused or inadequate, or I wouldn't have slapped that up on the mirror. I also keep in my wallet a yellowed note my dad wrote me many years ago. It says that I am special, that I am wise, and that he loves me. No matter what I've failed to do on any given day, no matter how inadequate someone has made me feel, every time I read that note I feel great. Feeling strong about yourself is what you'll need, because life and your own reaction to it may knock you off balance. Find some message, some thought, some prayer that helps you get there, and use it to get your strength back, your self back.

— *Maria Shriver*

Words to Remember When You're Wondering, "How Will I Ever Get Through This?"

People are like tea bags. You find out how strong they are when you put them in hot water.

— Author Unknown

Boil it all down to what counts the most: What is the essence of what you are trying to do, what is the most important thing? Things only get complicated when you are trying to address too many issues.

— Audrey Hepburn

*M*y advice: When juggling as much as you are, remember that some balls are glass and some are rubber. You can't drop the glass balls. Also, learn to put on blinders about certain things. Laundry will wait very patiently.

— *Nora Roberts*

*K*eep yourself clean and bright;
you are the window through which
you must see the world.

— *George Bernard Shaw*

You Hold the Key to Making This...

*B*e yourself.
Everyone else is already taken.

— *Oscar Wilde*

I've got something to say to you, and I hope you will listen with an open heart. Don't be so worried about what everybody else thinks of you, and don't think your happiness depends on someone else. I want you to just trust yourself. Trust that if you take care of yourself on the inside, follow your instincts, and let yourself evolve naturally, your potential for happiness will be so much greater.

— *Trisha Yearwood*

...a Happy, Healthy Journey

I am a woman in progress. I'm just
trying like everyone else. I try to take
every conflict, every experience and
learn from it. All I know is that I can't
be anybody else. And it's taken me a
long time to realize that.

— *Oprah Winfrey*

*I*t takes a long time to become a
person. Longer than they tell you.
Longer than I thought. I am grateful
for my past; it has given me the present.
I want to do well by the future.

— *Candice Bergen*

$\mathcal{T}$omorrow is a beautiful road that will take you right where you want to go... if you spend today walking away from worry and moving toward serenity, leaving behind conflict and traveling toward solutions, and parting with emptiness and never giving up on your search for fulfillment. If you can do what works for you, your present will be happier and your path will be smoother. And best of all?

You'll be taking a step into a beautiful future.

— *Douglas Pagels*

*A*mazing how we can light tomorrow with today.

— *Elizabeth Barrett Browning*

*S*ometimes the paths we take are long and hard, but remember: those are often the ones that lead to the most beautiful views. Have the courage to make that journey. And don't put limits on yourself. Too many dreams are waiting to be realized. Decisions are too important to leave to chance. Reach for your peak, your goal, your prize.

— *Douglas Pagels*

It All Starts with a Wish

*M*aybe there's something you want to change about your life. Or a dream you want to make come true.

It all starts with a wish.

It can be one like simply wanting to be a better person. Or it can be one of many other wonderful things. Maybe you want to be healthier, happier, lighter, a little less stressed-out, or much more in control of your life. Maybe there's something wrong that definitely needs to be right.

Maybe you want to make a change, but you're wondering if you really can. When you're feeling a little uncertain, you need to remember: if you can just make the commitment to change, if you can give yourself that hope and that gift, then I promise you this...

The happier and stronger person you are going to be in the days ahead will someday say a very precious thanks... for the decision that was made... by the person you are today.

And it's not that hard. It all starts with a wish. A wish turns into a step. A step turns into a path. And before you know it, you're on a beautiful journey that leads in the right direction. That's how you make your dreams come true. And that's how you discover what it's like to be every wonderful thing you were meant to be.

The future holds so much promise... if you keep holding on to your dreams.

— *Douglas Pagels*

Your Sweetest Dreams Are Closer Than You Know...

*E*ven if you can't just snap your fingers and make a dream come true, you can travel in the direction of your dream every single day, and you can keep shortening the distance between the two of you.

— *Douglas Pagels*

*T*he first step is what counts. First beginnings are hardest to make... but once they are made, it is easy to add the rest.

— *Aristotle*

*W*hen you are halfway there, you stop disbelieving in there.

— *Hugh Prather*

...Your Biggest Fears Are Smaller Than You Think

*F*ears are real only when we make them real by investing too much in them. When we allow fear to dominate our lives, we give it too much power....

Often, fear is the only thing that stands between us and our vision for a better life, and if you don't develop the courage to overcome those fears, you might never have the opportunity to reach your dreams and goals.

— Stedman Graham

$\mathscr{P}$romise yourself to be so strong that nothing can disturb your peace of mind...

Be too large for worry, too noble for anger, too strong for fear, and too happy to permit the presence of trouble.

— *Christian D. Larson*

$\mathscr{T}$he ability to focus and stay mentally tough comes with time and experience. You must learn to differentiate between what is truly important and what can be dealt with at another time. Maturity gives you the ability to prioritize.

— *Mia Hamm*

$\mathcal{I}$ try to separate my life into have-tos and should-dos.

— *Shaquille O'Neal*

$\mathcal{S}$ tress comes from doing things you don't want to do.

— *Author Unknown*

$\mathcal{T}$ ension is who you think you should be. Relaxation is who you are.

— *Chinese proverb*

*L*ife is a succession of lessons which must be lived to be understood.

— *Ralph Waldo Emerson*

*I*t helped me to read somewhere that there are no mistakes, only lessons. No problems, only opportunities.

— *Alice Walker*

I am grateful for all my problems. As each of them was overcome, I became stronger and more able to meet those yet to come. I grew on my difficulties.

— *J. C. Penney*

*W*ithout winter, there can be no spring. Without mistakes, there can be no learning. Without doubts, there can be no faith. Without fears, there can be no courage.

My mistakes, my fears, and my doubts are my path to wisdom, faith, and courage.

— *Author Unknown*

*I*n the midst of winter, I finally learned that there was in me an invincible summer.

— *Albert Camus*

Find Comfort in Knowing You Can Stay Safe and Warm...

The older I get, the more aware I become of the ebb and flow of certain feelings in my life. I know, for instance, to save certain things for the times when my inner strength is like a steady wind — filling the sails to take me where I need to go.

Some tasks ask me to wait for a better day, until I've got plenty of energy to get where I'm going, or to wait until my confidence is stronger. I may delay a difficult call that must be made, a visit that requires my happiest face, or a duty that demands an abundance of courage.

If I can wait until the time is right, I find I'm more likely to get to my destination.

— *Douglas Pagels*

...Till Any Storms Blow Over

I am not afraid of storms,
for I am learning
how to sail my ship.

— *Louisa May Alcott*

*T*here are some things
you learn best in calm,
some in storm.

— *Willa Cather*

*L*ife is a river, and we all have
to find a boat that floats.

— *Thad Carhart*

Find Strength in Your Hope

*A*t times you will find it hard
to bring forth your courage,
but at the bottom of your heart,
never give up hope.

— *Paul Cézanne*

*T*he more a diamond is cut,
the more it sparkles.

— *Author Unknown*

*H*ope has always allowed for all things.
Hope has always been there.

— *Amy Tan*

*H*ope in the face of difficulty. Hope in the face of uncertainty.

The audacity of hope! In the end, that is God's greatest gift to us... a belief in things not seen. A belief that there are better days ahead.

— *Barack Obama*

This Is One Thing
I'm Sure About

There are times in life when just being brave is all you need to be.

We may not always know what to do next... or how to get where we're going in life, but if we just stay strong, trust in our faith, and make the very best choices we possibly can, a few things may not go as planned... but almost everything else will work out right.

— *Douglas Pagels*

$\mathcal{A}$ bold heart is half the battle.

— *Author Unknown*

$\mathcal{L}$ook well into thyself; there is a source of strength which will always spring up if thou wilt always look there.

— *Marcus Aurelius*

$\mathcal{W}$hat lies behind us and what lies before us are tiny matters compared to what lies within us.

— *Ralph Waldo Emerson*

$\mathcal{S}$ometimes life deals you
blows that can knock you to
your knees. But no matter what
happens, we all have to get up
and move forward. Life goes on.

— *Venus Williams*

$\mathcal{T}$he world breaks everyone, and afterwards many are strong at the broken places.

— *Ernest Hemingway*

$\mathcal{L}$earn to bend. It's better than breaking.

— *Author Unknown*

$\mathcal{T}$o have courage for whatever comes in life — everything lies in that.

— *Saint Teresa of Avila*

$\mathcal{W}$hat a new face courage puts on everything!

— *Ralph Waldo Emerson*

Strength and Inspiration Come From...

A hero... is an ordinary individual who finds the strength to persevere and endure in spite of overwhelming obstacles.

— *Christopher Reeve*

*O*nly when something terrible happens, something that reminds us how precious life is, how short and fragile, only then are we able to see what really is — and isn't — important. Only then do we get the gift... of perspective.

— *Patti LaBelle*

...Those Who Face Difficulty Every Day

A single moment of understanding can flood a whole life with meaning.

— *Author Unknown*

*T*he answer was clear. After all that I'd been through, after all that I'd learned and all that I'd been given, I was going to do what I had been doing every day for the last few years now: just show up and do the best that I could with whatever lay in front of me.

— *Michael J. Fox*

$\mathcal{M}$any years ago, at the 1976 Seattle Special Olympics, the contestants, all physically or mentally disabled, assembled at the starting line for the 100-yard dash. At the gun, they all started out, not exactly in a dash, but with a relish to run the race to the finish and win.

All, that is, except one little boy who stumbled on the asphalt, tumbled over a couple of times, and began to cry. Some of the others heard the boy cry. Two of the runners slowed down, then they both turned around and went back.

One girl with Down syndrome bent down and kissed him and said, "This will make it better." Then the three linked arms and walked together to the finish line.

Everyone in the stadium stood, and the cheering went on for several minutes. People who were there are still telling the story.

Why? Because deep down we know this one thing: what matters in this life is more than winning for ourselves. What matters is helping others win, too, even if it means slowing down and changing our course.

— *Author Unknown*

Sometimes Our Guiding Lights...

*M*y grandma... told me once that happiness isn't on the road to anything. That happiness is the road.

— *Bob Dylan*

I am going your way, so let us go hand in hand. You help me and I'll help you. We shall not be here very long... so let us help one another while we may.

— *William Morris*

...Are Other People in Our Lives

Go beyond yourself and reach out to other people with a sincere love, respect, caring, and understanding of their needs.

— *Susan Polis Schutz*

We are each of us angels with only one wing. And we can only fly by embracing each other.

— *Luciano De Creschenzo*

Find Strength in Your Faith

I act as if everything depends upon me
and pray as if everything depends on God.

— *Oprah Winfrey*

*P*rayer is the golden key which should open
up the morning and lock up the evening.

— *Bishop Hopkins*

$\mathcal{T}$o me, faith means not worrying.

— *John Dewey*

$\mathcal{I}$'ve always heard that God never gives us more than we can handle.

— *Reba McEntire*

$\mathcal{H}$ave courage for the great sorrows of life and patience for the small ones; and when you have laboriously accomplished your daily task, go to sleep in peace. God is awake.

— *Victor Hugo*

Thoughts About Changes and New Beginnings

I know you're wondering what will happen in the next chapter of your life.

It isn't always easy to make changes, but there's no better advice than this: just do your best. Make sure you stay strong enough to move ahead because there are some wonderful rewards waiting for you.

It won't all make sense right away, but I promise you: over the course of time, answers will come, decisions will prove to be the right ones, and the path will be easier to see. Here are some things you can do that will help to see you through...

You can have hope. Because it works wonders for those who have it. You can be optimistic. Because people who expect things to turn out for the best often set the stage to receive a beautiful result.

You can put things in perspective. Because some things are important, and others are definitely not.

You can remember that beyond the clouds the sun is still shining. You can meet each challenge and give it all you've got.

You can count your blessings. You can be inspired to climb your ladders and have some nice, long talks with your wishing stars. You can be strong and patient. You can be gentle and wise.

And you can believe in happy endings. Because you are the author of the story of your life.

— Douglas Pagels

Create a Bright Tomorrow and Look Forward to...

I have hope and, with that, a determination to change what is not right. As a storyteller, I know that if I don't like the ending, I can write a better one.

— *Amy Tan*

The best way to predict the future is to create it.

— *Author Unknown*

Look at life through the windshield. Not the rearview mirror.

— *Author Unknown*

...How Good It's Going to Be

I always advise people to *clean the windshield* before you set out for your goals. By that, I mean for you to make sure you can clearly see where you want to go....

Clean the windshield to make sure that you are living according to the beliefs, principles, and values that you most want to guide your life.

— *Stedman Graham*

Find Strength in Being the Right Kind of Person...

There are two kinds of people in the world: those who come into a room and say, "Here I am!" and those who come in and say, "Ah, there you are!"

— *Author Unknown*

...and Spend Time with the Right Kind of People

*R*emember that a little love
    goes a long way.
Remember that a lot... goes forever.
Remember that friendship
    is a wise investment.
Life's treasures are people... together.

— Douglas Pagels

Strength Can Come...

$\mathcal{I}$ must say, I was blessed to find myself surrounded by all these very wise and loving women. Each had known what it was to live life, as well as to feel pain and heartache. With them I can speak freely....

They helped ease me into my new reality as painlessly and shamelessly as possible, pointing out the bumps in the road so I might fall fewer times and trip less.

— Fran Drescher

...from Friends

A friend is...

Someone who is concerned with everything
you do ⚬ someone to call upon during good
and bad times ⚬ someone who understands
whatever you do ⚬ someone who tells you the
truth about yourself ⚬ someone who knows
what you are going through at all times ⚬
someone who does not compete with you ⚬
someone who is genuinely happy for you when
things go well ⚬ someone who tries to cheer
you up when things don't go well ⚬ someone
who is an extension of yourself without which
you are not complete ⚬

— *Susan Polis Schutz*

...and Loved Ones

When you're scared or hurt or lonely, only one thing matters. People. Those you love and those who love you. The people you can count on to hold your hand, to see you through.

— *Patti LaBelle*

People must believe in each other, and feel that it can be done and must be done; in that way we are enormously strong. We must keep up each other's courage.

— *Vincent van Gogh*

...and Family

 $\mathcal{T}$ his path we are on is unpredictable, mysterious, profoundly challenging, and yes, even fulfilling. It is a path we chose to embark on together and for all the brambles and obstructions that have come our way of late, I have no regrets. In fact, all of our difficulties have shown me how deeply I love you and how grateful I am that we can follow this path together.

— *Dana Reeve*
(in a letter to Christopher Reeve
on their fourth wedding anniversary,
eleven months after Chris's accident)

Words to Help You Through Any Hard Times

Sometimes the news we receive can change everything so completely. The world around us seems to go on without realizing how much our hearts can be breaking... and without taking into account how vulnerable we suddenly feel. Life has a way of teaching us lessons we didn't necessarily want to learn... and giving us tests we never planned to take.

When you find yourself in a situation like this, I want you to be able to come to a place of comfort in your life. A place where you have a choice of feeling discouraged and worried and afraid... or being strong and steady and okay... and you put all your energy and faith in the path that is positive and in the choice that will help you heal.

If you can do that, you'll be able to get through any difficulty that comes along.

Eventually, the hurt won't hurt as much. And over the course of time, you will be touched with the reassuring recognition that "yes," you made it through. A little older and a little wiser, maybe… but with a lot of thanks to your strength, to your faith, and to the wonderful qualities that will always shine in you.

— *Douglas Pagels*

There's No Getting Around It: Sadness Comes to Us All...

*T*here's no way around grief and loss: you can dodge all you want, but sooner or later you just have to go into it, through it, and, hopefully, come out the other side. The world you find there will never be the same as the world you left.

— *Johnny Cash*

*W*hatever you are trying to avoid won't go away until you confront it.

— *Author Unknown*

*P*ain is inevitable.
Suffering is optional.

— *Author Unknown*

...But How Long It Stays Around Is Up to You

We all have our trials to bear in this life and mine have been considerable. But if the saying is true that living well is the best revenge, I have achieved my goals and then some. Each day, when I get up in the morning, put on my legs, and face a new day, I feel like one of the luckiest women in the world.

> — *Jami Goldman*
> *(world-class athlete, motivational*
> *speaker, and double amputee)*

I know that my life will never be all good or all bad. But if I'm lucky and continue to pour my heart into it, I'll have more good than bad.

And if I'm very lucky, I'll know it.

> — *Michelle Kwan*

Stay Strong While You're Waiting...

I know that whatever is making me feel bad is not going to last forever unless I allow it to.

— *Diana Ross*

*T*he most important thing in our lives is what we are doing now.

— *Author Unknown*

...for Time to Do Its Thing

As you dodge these curve balls that are coming at you now, don't let anyone take away your hope, get you down, or make you give up...

Refresh your spirit with the lessons you've learned. This is just a passage you're going through. You know your heart. You know who you are. There will be answers. Just be patient.

— *Donna Fargo*

Patience is the best remedy for every trouble.

— *Plautus*

I know I may never wind up living on "Easy Street," but if *Easier Street* ever becomes an option, I'm ready to make the move.

— *Douglas Pagels*

T here are times when life isn't all you want, but it's all you have. So what I say is, Have it! Stick a geranium in your hat and be happy!

— *Author Unknown*

M ake each new morning the opening door to a better day than the one before.

— *Author Unknown*

$\mathcal{W}$e've all used that expression "I've got a bone to pick with you." Somewhere along the way I learned an old folk saying that always seemed to me to be an interesting variation on that expression, but one which I think packs a lot of truth. If you want to succeed in life, the saying goes, you must pick three bones to carry with you at all times: a wishbone, a backbone, and a funnybone.

Those are three "bones" I always carry with me.

My wishes and dreams have always driven me forward over the biggest bumps and deepest potholes.

My stubborn, "no-quit" philosophy keeps my nerve strong at all times.

And, perhaps, most important of all, I make sure to keep a sense of humor and perspective about things, and I try to make sure laughter fills every day.

— *Reba McEntire*

Try Not to Worry

Don't tell me that worry doesn't do any good. I know better. The things I worry about don't happen.

— Author Unknown

Nothing wastes more energy than worrying. The longer one carries a problem, the heavier it gets. Don't take things too seriously. Live a life of serenity, not a life of regrets.

— Douglas Pagels

Worry gives a small thing a big shadow.

— Author Unknown

$\mathcal{K}$eep your face to the sunshine
and you cannot see the shadow.

— *Helen Keller*

$\mathcal{Y}$ou only live once, but if you
work it right, once is enough.

— *Joe E. Lewis*

$\mathcal{E}$ach day comes bearing
its gifts. Untie the ribbons.

— *Ann Schabacker*

Avoid Wrong Turns and Dangerous Detours

I have lost a lot of friends... they became addicted to various substances. They could never feel how far was too far. They thought that they could handle anything, stay in control of the substances that were making them feel invincible, that were egging them on to cross any boundary....

We always have an "it won't happen to me" attitude when we see other people making mistakes. Don't be fooled. It can happen to you — if you aren't careful, if you don't know who you are — anything can happen.

— *Queen Latifah*

$\mathcal{W}$e need the courage
to start and continue
what we should do
and the courage to stop
what we shouldn't do.

— *Richard L. Evans*

$\mathcal{M}$aking a mistake doesn't mean it's all
over. It doesn't mean you quit and live off
that as an excuse for not being successful.
You use that mistake as a springboard to
becoming successful.

— *Montel Williams*

$\mathcal{S}$ometimes it is by making a mistake
that one finds the right road.

— *Vincent van Gogh*

All You Need to Be Is Strong Enough...

Anyone can carry his burden, however hard, until nightfall. Anyone can do his work, however hard, for one day. Anyone can live sweetly, patiently, lovingly, purely, till the sun goes down. And this is all life really means.

— *Robert Louis Stevenson*

...to Make It Through the Day

Having spent the better part of my life trying either to relive the past or experience the future before it arrives, I have come to believe that in between these two extremes is peace.

— *Author Unknown*

There are such beautiful possibilities in a life that is taken one day at a time.

— *Douglas Pagels*

It's Never Too Late to Have...

*M*ost of us miss out on life's big prizes.
The Pulitzer. The Nobel. Oscars. Tonys.
Emmys. But we're all eligible for life's small
pleasures. A pat on the back. A kiss behind
the ear. A four-pound bass. A full moon.
An empty parking space. A crackling fire.
A great meal. A glorious sunset…

Don't fret about copping life's grand awards.
Enjoy its tiny delights. There are plenty for
all of us.

— *Author Unknown*

A life well lived is simply a compilation
of days well spent.

— *Douglas Pagels*

...These Wonderful Realizations

*W*hat a wonderful life I've had!
I only wish I'd realized it sooner.

— *Colette*

*L*ife isn't a dress rehearsal. We don't get any do-overs. You've got to make the days count — all of them....

And at the end of every day, ask yourself if you have any regrets. I guarantee you, you will rarely regret the things you did do, and mostly regret the things you didn't do. So do it. Do it all. Learn French. Get a piano. Write your one-person show. Fall in love more often. Love the journey, not just the result.

— *Camryn Manheim*

Don't Ever Forget How Special You Really Are

As you go through life, try to remember these gentle words of reassurance...

"I know there will be days when I may be less than some people prefer me to be, but most people are unaware that I am so much more than what they see."

— *Douglas Pagels*

"Tigger is all right really," said Piglet lazily. "Of course he is," said Christopher Robin. "Everybody is really," said Pooh.

— *A. A. Milne*

*T*hey are able who think they are able.

— *Virgil*

*E*verything nourishes what is strong already.

— *Jane Austen*

*P*erhaps I am stronger than I think.

— *Thomas Merton*

Stay Strong...

I have found recovery, joy, tremendous gratitude, and the knowledge that the stars are always shining somewhere. I have only to look through the blue sky or into the black night to find them and let them shine on me. The sky will clear, my mind will clear, if I move from negative to positive. In the moment of silence between stars, there is healing, there is the sound of the pulse of light, the sound of God talking to me, listening to me, healing me, bringing me strength. All I have to do is look up.

— *Judy Collins*

$\mathcal{N}$o star is ever lost we once have seen,
we may always be what we might have been.

— Adelaide A. Proctor

$\mathcal{I}$ finally feel whole — connected to
both the past and the present, the
living and the lost. The world has many
edges, and all of us dangle from them
by a very delicate thread. The key is
not to let go.

— Anderson Cooper

...Hold On

I know not what the future holds,
but I know who holds the future.

— *Author Unknown*

...and Hang In There

It takes a strong person to deal with tough times and difficult choices. But you are a strong person. It takes courage. But you possess the inner courage to see you through. It takes being an active participant in your life. But you are in the driver's seat, and you can determine the direction you want tomorrow to go in.

Hang in there... and take care to see that you don't lose sight of the one thing that is constant, beautiful, and true: Everything will be fine — and it will turn out that way because of the special kind of person you are.

So... beginning today and lasting a lifetime through — hang in there, and don't be afraid to feel like the stars are shining... just for you.

— *Douglas Pagels*

ACKNOWLEDGMENTS

We gratefully acknowledge the permission granted by the following authors, publishers, and authors' representatives to reprint poems or excerpts from their publications.

Grand Central Publishing for "I keep a little saying on my mirror..." from TEN THINGS I WISH I'D KNOWN – BEFORE I WENT OUT INTO THE REAL WORLD by Maria Shriver. Copyright © 2000 by Maria Shriver. Reprinted by permission of Grand Central Publishing. All rights reserved. And for "Only when something..." and "When you're scared or hurt..." from PATTI'S PEARLS by Patti LaBelle. Copyright © 2001 by Patti LaBelle and Laura Randolph Lancaster. Reprinted by permission of Grand Central Publishing. All rights reserved. And for "I must say, I was blessed to find myself..." from CANCER SCHMANCER by Fran Drescher. Copyright © 2002 by Fran Drescher. Reprinted by permission of Grand Central Publishing. All rights reserved.

Atria Books, an imprint of Simon & Schuster Adult Publishing Group, for "Boil it all down to..." by Audrey Hepburn from AUDREY HEPBURN: AN ELEGANT SPIRIT by Sean Hepburn Ferrer. Copyright © 2003 by Sean Hepburn Ferrer. All rights reserved.

Broadway Books, a division of Random House, Inc., for "My advice: When juggling..." by Nora Roberts, "I've got something to say..." by Trisha Yearwood, and "Life isn't a dress rehearsal..." by Camryn Manheim from WHAT I KNOW, edited by Ellyn Spragins. Copyright © 2006 by Ellyn Spragins. All rights reserved.

John Wiley & Sons, Inc., for "I am a woman in progress..." and "I act as if everything..." from OPRAH WINFREY SPEAKS by Janet Lowe. Copyright © 1988 by Janet Lowe. All rights reserved.

Simon & Schuster Adult Publishing Group for "It takes a long time to become..." from KNOCK WOOD by Candice Bergen. Copyright © 1984 by Candice Bergen. All rights reserved. And for "Fears are real only when we make them..." and "I always advise people..." from YOU CAN MAKE IT HAPPEN by Stedman Graham. Copyright © 1997 by Graham-Williams Group. All rights reserved. And for "My grandma... told me once..." from CHRONICLES by Bob Dylan. Copyright © 2004 by Bob Dylan. All rights reserved.

Hugh Prather and Conari Press for "When you are halfway..." from LOVE AND COURAGE by Hugh Prather. Copyright © 2001 by Hugh Prather. All rights reserved.

HarperCollins Publishers for "The ability to focus and stay..." from GO FOR THE GOAL by Mia Hamm and Aaron Heifetz. Copyright © 1999 by Mia Hamm. All rights reserved. And for "There's no way around grief..." from CASH: THE AUTOBIOGRAPHY by Johnny Cash and Patrick Carr. Copyright © 1997 by John R. Cash. All rights reserved. And for "I have lost a lot of friends..." from LADIES FIRST by Queen Latifah and Karen Hunter. Copyright © 1999 by Queen Latifah, Inc. All rights reserved. And for "I finally feel whole..." from DISPATCHES FROM THE EDGE by Anderson Cooper. Copyright © 2006 by Anderson Cooper. All rights reserved.

St. Martin's Press for "I try to separate my life..." from SHAQ TALKS BACK by Shaquille O'Neal. Copyright © 2001 by Mine-O-Mine, Inc. All rights reserved.

Hyperion for "The answer was clear..." from LUCKY MAN by Michael J. Fox. Copyright © 2002 by Michael J. Fox. Reprinted by permission. All rights reserved.

Scribner, an imprint of Simon & Schuster Adult Publishing Group, and Wendy Weil Agency for "It helped me to read..." from THE SAME RIVER TWICE: HONORING THE DIFFICULT by Alice Walker. Copyright © 1996 by Alice Walker. All rights reserved.

Random House Trade Paperbacks, a division of Random House, Inc., for "Life is a river..." from THE PIANO SHOP ON THE LEFT BANK by Thad Carhart. Copyright © 2001 by T. E. Carhart. All rights reserved.

G.P. Putnam's Sons, a division of Penguin Group (USA), Inc., and Sandra Dijkstra Literary Agency for "Hope has always allowed..." and "I have hope and..." from THE OPPOSITE OF FATE by Amy Tan. Copyright © 2003 by Amy Tan. All rights reserved.

Three Rivers Press, a division of Random House, Inc., and Jane Dystel Literary Management for "Hope in the face of difficulty" from DREAMS FROM MY FATHER by Barack Obama. Copyright © 1995, 2004 by Barack Obama. All rights reserved.

Houghton Mifflin Company for "Sometimes life deals you..." by Venus Williams from VENUS AND SERENA: SERVING FROM THE HIP by Venus Williams and Serena Williams. Copyright © 2005 by Venus Williams and Serena Williams. All rights reserved.

Ballantine Books, a division of Random House, Inc., for "A hero...is an ordinary..." from STILL ME by Christopher Reeve. Copyright © 1998 by Cambria Productions, Inc. All rights reserved.

Bantam Books, a division of Random House, Inc., for "I've always heard that God never..." and "We've all used that expression..." from COMFORT FROM A COUNTRY QUILT by Reba McEntire. Copyright © 1999 by Reba McEntire. All rights reserved. Random House, Inc., for "This path we are on is..." from CARE PACKAGES by Dana Reeve. Copyright © 1999 by Cambria Productions, Inc. All rights reserved.

Simon & Schuster Adult Publishing Group and Paul Fedorko Agency for "We all have our trials..." from UP AND RUNNING by Jami Goldman and Andrea Cagan. Copyright © 2001 by Jami Goldman. All rights reserved.

Scholastic, Inc., for "I know that my life will never..." from HEART OF A CHAMPION by Michelle Kwan. Copyright © 1997 by Michelle Kwan Corp. All rights reserved.

Villard Books, a division of Random House, Inc., for "I know that whatever is making me..." from SECRETS OF A SPARROW by Diana Ross. Copyright © 1993 by Diana Ross. All rights reserved.

PrimaDonna Entertainment Corp. for "As you dodge these curve balls..." from I PRAYED FOR YOU TODAY by Donna Fargo. Copyright © 2005 by PrimaDonna Entertainment Corp. All rights reserved.

Hazelden Publishing and Education for "We need the..." by Richard L. Evans from NIGHT LIGHT: A BOOK OF NIGHTTIME MEDITATIONS by Amy E. Dean. Copyright © 1986 by Hazelden Foundation, Center City, MN. All rights reserved.

Hay House, Inc., Carlsbad, California, for "Making a mistake..." from LIFE LESSONS AND REFLECTIONS by Montel Williams. Copyright © 2000 by Montel Williams. All rights reserved.

Dutton Children's Books, a division of Penguin Young Readers Group, a Member of Penguin Group (USA), Inc., 345 Hudson Street, New York, NY 10014, for "Tigger is all right..." from THE HOUSE AT POOH CORNER by A. A. Milne, Illustrations by E. H. Shepard, copyright 1928 by E. P. Dutton, renewed © 1956 by A. A. Milne. All rights reserved.

Jeremy P. Tarcher, an imprint of Penguin Group (USA), Inc., for "I have found recovery, joy..." from SANITY AND GRACE by Judy Collins. Copyright © 2003 by Judy Collins. All rights reserved.

A careful effort has been made to trace the ownership of selections used in this anthology in order to obtain permission to reprint copyrighted material and give proper credit to the copyright owners. If any error or omission has occurred, it is completely inadvertent, and we would like to make corrections in future editions provided that written notification is made to the publisher:

BLUE MOUNTAIN ARTS, INC., P.O. Box 4549, Boulder, Colorado 80306.